A Church Musician Muses

upon Her Life and Work

A Church Musician Muses
upon Her Life and Work

by

Elsie Pauline Naylor

ZION PUBLISHING
Des Moines, Iowa

Cover photo by Edwards Picture Parlor

Back cover photo by Lifetouch

About the Cover: Elsie Pauline Naylor, b. 1938, is pictured at the console of the Casavant organ in the sanctuary of Immanuel United Methodist Church, Des Moines, IA in June 1979. Elsie's parents, Hoyt and Maxine Naylor, met and were married at Immanuel when the church was in its early beginnings. She and her brothers, Ray and Earl, were raised in this congregation. The current sanctuary was built in 1968 and the Casavant installed the same year. Ms Naylor returned from her position in Winona, MN to play the dedicatory recital in the fall of 1968.

ISBN-978-0-9979841-7-0

Zion Publishing
Des Moines IA

DEDICATION

This book is lovingly dedicated to my
parents, Hoyt and Maxine Naylor.
Their support of my service playing,
programs and recitals was never-failing.

The Sparrow

This was a familiar trade with my neighbor. "I'm going away for a few days." Eleanor called out. "Will you take care of my plants?"

The only thing different this time was her suggestion that the two big planters be carried over to my deck porch so I wouldn't have to open up her house every day to water them. On the fourth morning of this arrangement, I again put the slender spout of the watering can into the pink geranium plant and suddenly was met with a flutter and sputter as a baby bird descended to the bench on which the plant sat. "I'm sorry, I didn't know you were in there!" I apologized as I jumped back.

Let's be clear from the beginning, I am not a bird person. I acknowledge the animal kingdom as part of

God's good creation, but the cat is the only one I really like. I was always glad that my father was the one who disposed of those tiny baby kittens who didn't survive birth or took the old cats to the veterinarian when they were too sick to live any longer. No messiness for me, thank you.

And now, here was this tiny bird, rudely ousted from its nest and completely helpless. Hindsight says I should have replaced it in the nest or, my squeamish nature being what it is, found someone who could do it. But I left it huddled close to the planter and retreated behind the sliding glass door to my safe nest, where I could observe and ponder the situation.

I prayed to whatever part of God's spirit takes care of this kind of creature. I mentally talked to the mother bird, which perched on the rain spout and called and called for her baby, apparently not seeing how close it was to her. I gave thanks when the adult birds did find the little one a couple of times and fed it. Life calling to life: Please, let it live.

Knowing I had other tasks to do in addition to observing a little bird, I checked my appointment calendar and was reminded that this was the birthday of my friend Ruth. Or it would have been. A year and a half before this saga on my deck, Ruth shot and killed her husband and herself. He had Alzheimer's disease; she felt that in earlier years they had agreed never to go to a nursing home. I suppose the plan must have rooted and grown in her mind for a long time. This was not the first time I had experienced grief, but I wasn't prepared for the emotions of horror, disbelief, and anger that came at the news of her death. Especially the anger.

Although she was several years my senior, we had been close friends for twenty-five years. We shared not only the everyday concerns of family and work but especially the insights and help we received in our spiritual journeys. Then all the sharing was gone, all the opportunities for help and counsel no longer possible.

It seems easy to be compassionate about an unknown suicide victim. How much more difficult it is to deal with personal feelings, to realize that forgiveness often happens in small increments rather than with one grand gesture. Has the time come to let go of all the "whys" and "what ifs," and let peace come in their place? Life calling to Life, and more than that, Life calling us to Love.

How was the bird to survive the night? I soaked some bread cubes in milk and put the mixture in a shallow lid close to the planter. I put some seeds and bread crust on a paper plate on the bench in hopes of attracting the adult birds. I mentally wrapped the planter and baby bird in the Light and went to bed.

The next morning I opened the curtains and saw only the planter. Quickly moving to the kitchen window, I saw that the bird had moved to the other side – it's alive! I made innumerable trips to the window during the day, taking a lesson from cats on how quietly and carefully one must move in order not to frighten the birds. Same means, different motive! Late afternoon, and no bird. I even ventured out on the deck just to be sure. The flooring of the deck is made up of 1x6 boards, spaced about an inch apart. Oh my, the bird must have flopped off the bench and onto the floor.

I gingerly walked around, trying to peer between the boards. No sign of it. I entertained the idea that perhaps birds know what humans ponder: how to leave this earth without going through the process of death. This noble thought was soon abandoned when the mother bird again appeared, first on the rain spout and then the bench, calling and calling for her young. No response.

A short time later the male bird came on the scene, hopping on the floor, calling and putting his head between the boards. He certainly pinpointed the spot for me – and we both heard the faint chirp of the baby bird. Eleanor was now back in town, so I had someone close by to help me decide what to do. She came with a lanky teen-age grandson in tow who was strong enough to lift up the wooden pallet. Sure enough, there was the bird in the corner, and the boy deftly gathered it in his hands. Some choices don't seem all that life-giving: to leave the bird on my deck meant it would probably get caught again in the boards and die for sure; to move the planter and bird back to Eleanor's porch didn't guarantee life unless the adult birds would find the nest again. Opting for that possibility, the procession returned next door.

My life was in turmoil at the time of the bird episode. A few months before, I felt the need to resign from my 28-year position as director of music/organist at a large United Methodist Church. I had not found other employment and was still waiting for replies to job applications. It was a challenge to keep a positive attitude and truly believe that I would be guided to the best place for me to serve. What kind of a message did I receive as an answer to my prayers? A bird that needed to get back to its nest and the memory of a dear friend whom I had not yet completely forgiven.

Actually, there was another answer: a melody and words from an old gospel hymn had been playing in my mind since I found the bird. That might not be shocking to a number of church-goers, but it was an eye-opener to this classically trained church musician who was taught that most of the 19th century gospel hymns should be left in that century. After all, those hymns were written in a simplistic text and musical style meant to solicit an altar call from the congregants who were singing them. As mainline worship leaders in the mid-20th century, we discouraged the use of these hymns. My discovery of inclusive language changed other hymns or eliminated them as a choice, but there were still several centuries from which we could find uplifting texts and tunes.

Worship leaders may have set the old gospel hymns aside, but I doubt that many worshippers in the pews did so. Whatever the style of music, the songs from our early experiences in church remain with us as adults. If those songs are also associated with a religious experience or conversion, there is no doubt they remain our favorites. I'm glad that my "favorites" cover a span of several centuries. The different musical styles and texts resonate with the variety of my spiritual experiences and beliefs. However, I remain a tad amused at the cosmic humor that sent the answer to my prayers in the form of the old refrain:

I sing because I'm happy,
I sing because I'm free,
For His eye is on the sparrow,
And I know He watches me.

That watchfulness has continued as I found another church community in which I can share my gifts and skills of music and worship leadership. I am more and more aware of Grace, that unconditional love of God, and how it helps me discern the meaning of experiences in my life.

A kind editor asked me why I had not mentioned Ruth again as I came to the end of the story about the bird. Now, years later, as I rewrite this essay, I realize that somehow it was a bookmark, until the "fullness of time" when I could trust myself and God enough to re-examine the episode. Now, forgiveness can happen at a deeper level.

Now, I can realize that part of the memory I have been carrying all these years is rejection. I thought I was an integral part of Ruth's family, but I was not included in any of the preparations or discussions. I could neither give nor receive comfort—I was an outsider.

So there it is: a burden I had no idea I was carrying, and to recognize it is time to lay it down. Now I know the event will always be with me, but it is no longer the defining moment in my friendship with Ruth. She and I, and the baby bird and all creation, are forever held in unconditional Love.

Oh, yes. Eleanor saw the bird leave its nest a few days later.

(Original story written August 2-5, 1995.
Final revision 9/25/08)

Can't You Keep That Baby Quiet?

Does anyone really want to observe the Feast of the Holy Innocents on the 28th of December? The Gospel of Matthew gives us that terrible account of Herod ordering the slaughter of all male babies two years old and younger—children forever silenced. Matthew's quote from Jeremiah is bone chilling:

> A voice was heard in Ramah,
> wailing and loud lamentation,
> Rachel weeping for her children;
> she refused to be consoled,
> because they were no more.

The Christmas services have once more given us that sweet picture of the Babe and Holy family, adored by shepherds, magi and even the barn animals. Why would we want to hear about the killing of innocent children, let alone make it the theme of the day?

I have heard a baby cry in a worship service, or watched a small child's antics completely disrupt the concentration of adult worshippers, and have thought to myself, "Don't those parents realize how much their child is upsetting the flow of this worship service? Why don't they take the child out of the sanctuary?"

Let's be blunt: it may be easier to extol the virtues of children in worship when they aren't present in the service. We quickly rationalize that position by reminding ourselves that the worship service needs to be meaningful to adults. Finding elements a child can understand that still gives inspiration to adult worshippers is difficult. Instead of incorporating children in the service, perhaps we should just talk about the issues confronting children today. Hardly any research is needed in order to preach the Matthew text. We can easily find statistics about child abuse, poverty, neglect, and homelessness. Or we can just read the daily newspaper and find more than we would ever want to know about the condition of children in our society. The glut of information may numb our hearts and minds to the ever-present call of the gospel to take care of even "the least of these."

One summer Sunday, I was seated in a pew rather

than my usual place in the choir loft. It didn't take me long to realize there was more distraction or commotion among the congregation than in the slightly isolated chancel area. Just as quickly, I figured out that if I were to gain anything from the worship service that day, I needed to accept my fellow worshippers and their murmuring, even as I concentrated on the liturgy.

When the offering plates are passed at Urbandale United Church of Christ, it is the custom of the congregation for each member (child or adult) to hold the plate and offer prayers or intentions, whether or not a monetary gift is placed in the plate. At the time of the offering, I looked across the aisle and saw Kelsey, her legs swinging because they did not reach the floor, take a plate, hold it and bow her head before passing it to her mother.

Did Kelsey understand all the elements of the worship service that day? I doubt it. Did all of the adults in attendance understand all the elements of the service? Probably not. It is a challenge to worship leaders to discover ways that children may authentically participate and lead in worship. I have understood for years that the "children's time" or "children's sermon" often serves only to exploit our children. I have also been one of those who wished they were seen but not heard. How do we move in a direction that gives them their rightful voice? Congregations will find more than one way to achieve this. Our children deserve the best spiritual formation we can provide for them. My colleague in ministry recently made this observation: "I do not believe that our children are the future church. They are the present church! Their spiritual development may be at a different level than an adult member, but they are part of our church now."

I don't remember the sermon from the pulpit on that summer day several years ago. I do remember Kelsey's feet swinging as she prayed over the offering plate.

Requiem for a Handbell Ringer

There we were: seven young teenagers, a first year professional church musician, a newly donated two octave (25 notes) set of handbells, and a senior minister who thought this was going to be a great way to involve some of the youth in the church. Not necessarily a recipe for success. Teenagers were not my favorite age of music volunteer.

My opinion had been colored by one of my jobs while I was still in college. I was the assistant organist at a large Presbyterian church. This congregation was the city's shining example of the Westminster Choir College graded choir program (made popular in the first half of the 20th century), and it was still going strong in the middle 1960s. It fell to my lot to be accompanist for the junior high school choir, which was so large that it was divided into three rehearsal sections, each one with 30 to 40 singers. That's still too many sweaty, loud, hormone fluctuating, tired-from-a-day-at-school bodies to put together in one room. When my time at that church was over, I was convinced that teenagers were the last people I ever wanted to direct in a choir.

So, it was a delight to discover that teenagers, taken in small numbers, could be witty, smart, and a lot of fun. This first handbell choir and I set about the task of learning to ring bells. There was very little music commercially written for two octaves in those early years. Necessity forced me to remember techniques learned in college music arranging classes in order to come up with material my choir could play. Together, the teenagers and I made music.

This was a period of fewer demands on the time of children and youth, and I enjoyed the luxury of having them participate in choir for five or six years. The first group played until they graduated from high school. Then, almost imperceptibly, the change happened. First, they stayed only until their junior year, and then eventually there were fewer and fewer years committed to a choir. I don't believe that my congregation, or the Church at large, realized how much popular culture would attract—

and demand—from our youth in the later decades of the 20th century. Sports and part-time jobs were not very sympathetic to those who might have wanted to take one night a week for music practice. If the teenagers weren't willing to give every afternoon and evening to drills or work, then there were others waiting in line to take their place. Parents often felt torn between wanting their children to be involved in church activities and knowing that the young people needed to begin taking responsibility for making their own decisions.

I doubt that we could have prevented this shift, but I wonder how many of us really understand that the Church is not called to be popular, but counter-cultural. The message of extravagant love and hospitality, all of us beloved children of God, is a message that continues to challenge those of us who are professionally hired and called by the Church. How much more it must challenge teenagers who are trying to sort out that message while constantly being exposed to the popular ideas of winning at all costs and valuing some people more than others.

Children, youth and adults continued to play handbells. I left that position in 1995, and I confess that I no longer recall all the names of the ringers. However, reading my former city's newspaper online one day brought one name into quick recognition. "Michael Benson, age

40, left for Iraq on Easter weekend 2005, and died Aug. 10 from wounds sustained during an improvised explosive attack in Baghdad on Aug 2."

I had a number of bell choirs before Mike was old enough to join one. Two of his three older brothers had played in earlier groups, one of them in my first bell choir. Although none of the family had formal musical training, the boys had little difficulty handling the bells and music. I don't remember how many years Mike played in a choir, but I do have a picture of him in my mind as the only junior high boy in a group with six or seven girls of the same age. We prepared for the area festival that year—and he was the hit of the whole festival! He impressed the adults and wowed all the girls.

After Mike graduated from high school, he came to my office one day and asked if I would write a reference for him because he wanted to enlist in the Army. I reluctantly granted his request. I try to console myself with the idea that he would have joined whether or not I had given him a recommendation. I'm sure he had qualities that the armed forces appreciated.

I do have to wonder if I should have talked about the gospel message of nonviolence, if I should have helped him look for other ways to give to his country. A number of years ago I made the decision to eliminate "should" or "ought" from my vocabulary and thinking as much as possible, but the question of what I "should" have done for Mike lingers.

A church musician has many children, if not biological, then graciously loaned by their parents. I have watched and loved these children as they made the journey to young adulthood. I have observed their pain or happiness as they dealt with school, relationships, and questions of faith that their journey produced.

So I find myself with the same lament as birth parents: it is against the natural order for children to die before their parents! A drunken driver, breast cancer, bulimia, AIDS, and the Iraq war have taken five of my "children" who were hardly into the prime of their lives. These are causes that for the most part could have been prevented. Causes for which the 20th century should have found a cure but which still plague us in the 21st century.

My dear ringers, I mourn for you. I mourn for your families and friends. I mourn for the world, which will never know each of you and all the qualities that you might have offered us. And I thank God for the moments of time I shared with you. "Requiescat in pace" – rest in peace.

(7/19/2007)

That Was Just Delicious

The scene is familiar. Ten or fifteen minutes into the morning worship service the Minister sits down on the steps leading to the front chancel area of the sanctuary, trying to give the appearance of being totally relaxed even though seated in an uncomfortable position. Hoping to present a welcoming atmosphere, the minister asks, "Will the children come forward and join me for the Children's Sermon?"

The parade begins with the older elementary age children bravely walking or running to the steps, followed by the shy five and six year olds, and concludes with a couple of parents carrying the very reluctant three and four year olds who find it scary to be any place except in the pew close to a parent or other relative. During this time a murmur may float through the congregation as the adults take note of the antics of the children in the procession, or the cute way they are dressed. The anticipation continues to build as the minister gives a prepared sermonette, hopefully laying out the general idea of the morning theme and sermon in childlike terms.

Questions are posed to the children. If there is no response, everyone can find interest, if not delight, in observing the minister cover the awkward moment. But what is really hoped for is some comment made by a child in all earnestness, a comment that seems naïve and funny to adult minds. The congregation continues to smile as the children are dismissed back to their seats, and it is not uncommon to hear a parishioner comment at the end of the service, "I get more out of the Children's Time than any other part of the service."

"Entertainment Worship" is not a new thing, after all. For years, the innocent comments of children have been a diversion for adults who are either bored by the liturgy or who don't understand that corporate (communal) worship asks their active participation and not just passive observation. This has certainly been a topic of conversation for church staff members with whom I have worked, and I imagine it has been a common lament in numerous churches.

Are there other ways to include children in worship instead of a designated children's time? The staff of the last church I served wrestled with that dilemma for several months. Interestingly, it was a group of parents who wanted other choices, rather than the appearance of just putting the children on display on the chancel steps.

We decided to offer four opportunities each month. The Children's Choir sang one week. Another week the older children could help hand out bulletins or read a scripture lesson. The children had their own separate time during the service, so one Sunday a month they would create a prayer or other activity that could be shared with the rest of the congregation at the offertory. Since we celebrate communion once a month, on that day the children would be invited to come to the front of the Communion Table and observe as the minister led the first part of the ritual.

Do we dare trust little children to know how to act when they are standing around the Table, all of them curious, some of them barely tall enough to rest their chins on the table? They followed the minister's explanation about why we have communion, and they watched with interest when bread was broken and juice poured into the cup. It was not "entertainment" to watch them –

it was to see with fresh eyes again the awesome Mystery of communion, a mystery that adults often might take for granted.

A number of years ago, the United Methodist congregation which employed me had a general, but not hard and fast, guideline that children would not take communion. To give the parishioners a reason that communion elements be offered to children, one of our associate ministers told the story of watching his young daughter drawing a picture during the communion time. Not a drawing of a cup and bread, but a drawing of a heart! The minister concluded that his child did indeed understand the basic element in the ritual, that God's love is what it's all about.

One of the privileges of serving as a worship leader at Urbandale United Church of Christ was the opportunity for me to observe the members of the congregation as they came forward to take communion by intinction. As each one took a piece of bread and then dipped it in the cup, I was aware of various pastoral concerns. Health issues, emotional problems, joys and pains – the whole gamut of the human condition, coming forward in the form of older adults pushing walkers, a choir member stepping into the line to be with a spouse, parents with very young children in their arms.

Perhaps the most touching moment of all was to see the communion servers stoop down, holding the basket of bread and the cup at the level a child could reach: Unconditional Love being extended, whether one understands the words of the ritual or not.

Retirement has moved me from the chancel area to the pew, which is not always a happy adjustment. I have missed the leadership role. I also realized I missed the focus and quietness at the front of the church in the chancel area, as opposed to being distracted by the activity that goes on in the pews: adults being amused by the antics of children around them, whispered comments to one another about the order of service, people of all ages leaving the sanctuary and then coming back in whether or not it is an appropriate time. "Don't you people have any sense of a worship service?!" Fortunately, only my inner voice shouted this, and I have now become more comfortable with my place in my church family, foibles and all.

If I had chosen to move my membership to another congregation after my employment was over, I would have missed one of the most precious things I have ever heard a child utter in church. One Sunday, Taylor Hoover and her three children were seated behind me in the service. After they had returned from communion, little Sophia remarked, "That was just delicious!"

Her mother told me that Sophia's favorite part of the service is when she can dip the bread in the juice. Taylor went on to say, "Our Sophia is five years old and definitely an old soul. Communion is her favorite part of church. Sophia's full name is Sophia Jiovanina Annaleese Hoover. It means wisdom, God is gracious, grace and favor. I believe it is a perfect fit for my beautiful girl."

I have pondered that phrase many times; can't you hear the ripple of laughter that would have gone through the congregation if it had been uttered during a Children's Time? I'm glad that's not what happened. The words need to be contemplated over and over. The question that keeps coming to me is: Can you apply this to your whole life? Has this child just made a cute statement? Or has Sophia, the old soul, actually laid out a spiritual question that may probe deep into our own souls?

From ancient biblical writers, to theologians through the centuries, to contemporary scientists and students of the mind and psyche, all of them (all of us) seek to understand the human condition. We want to know how life and joy manifest, and why so many people have situations and afflictions that seem to deprive them of any good thing.

For myself, I find that the more seasons of life I celebrate, the less I can explain all that happens. I think this is not so much a discouragement in the spiritual life as it is an acknowledgement of how vast the universe of God is. I'm not a big fan of the writings of St. Paul, but I do find comfort in I Corinthians 13:12: "Now I know in part, then I shall understand fully, even as I have been fully understood." I hear again Sophia's statement, "That was just delicious!" Is it possible to come up to the end of this life on earth and be able to speak those words?

We're back to the Children's Time. In each of our lifetimes, I wonder how many other gems from God's thoughts to the lips of small children may have been lost because we only saw the "cuteness" of the children. It turns out that I only needed one thought in order to be changed and challenged. The question still remains, "Is it possible to come to the end of this lifetime and say, 'That was just delicious!'"?

I'm certainly not there yet in my own thinking, and I can call to mind numerous others who, because of their life experiences, could hardly be expected to utter that phrase. But Sophia persists, "That was just delicious!"

(Sophia's words are from December 2011.)
(Manuscript was finished January 7, 2014.)

The following two essays I found in my archives and assume they were written for church newsletters.

To Clap or not to Clap,
That is the question

Clapping, dancing, spontaneous vocal outbursts and the like are welcomed in some congregations and hotly debated as inappropriate in others. How do we encourage individual expression in a corporate setting? Can we appreciate diverse responses and yet acknowledge that not everyone will want to do the same thing? Can we have spontaneous responses without having them finally turn into perfunctory ritual? These two short essays are offered as reflection, not as final answers!

Amen Corner

Have you ever heard the phrase "the Amen corner?" It's been floating in my mind for a few days - the phrase, not the corner! I think it refers to the people in a congregation, perhaps in one corner or section of the room, who punctuate the various elements of the worship service with a very vocal "amen." Although this practice is still maintained in some denominations, I suspect that many of us are reluctant to add anything verbal that's not called for in the bulletin. I was reminded of this hesitance recently when I served as substitute organist for one of the large churches in town. The offertory music was a duet, "Every time I feel the Spirit." The voices were great, the singers enthusiastic, and the accompanist played an exciting piano style appropriate to this spiritual. And when the music stopped, the large room was silent.

For the most part, I have come to appreciate silence as an appropriate response to musical offerings, sermons, and other elements of worship. Silence gives us a moment to reflect on what we have just heard, to remember that worship leaders are offering their talents on behalf of all the congregation as a way of praising God. But when that spiritual finished, my soul cried, "Amen!" and my mouth remained silent. I excused myself by reasoning that since I was a guest there, I didn't know how that congregation usually responded. I struggle against shallow sentimentality in worship, but do I welcome honest emotion? The few times I have dared to utter an "Amen,"

I have been filled with joy and freedom. Yet I passed up a great opportunity to witness to my belief in the words of that spiritual.

Webster's dictionary defines amen as "used to express solemn ratification or hearty approval." Every time I feel the Spirit moving in my heart, I will pray. And I will laugh and cry and sing, and once in a while, I will say "Amen"- will you join me?

(7/21/96)

I Won't Dance, Don't Make Me

In one of my worship experiences this summer, I found myself unwilling to join some of my fellow worshippers in the enthusiastic clapping to one of the songs. Plainly put, I just wasn't in the mood, and I resented the implication from others that I wasn't really appreciating the music. Did I overreact? Probably. Did I learn something from the experience? Yes!

It has been liberating for me to discover that I can let my body move to some of the music in worship, or that it's OK to get excited enough about a sermon to offer an "amen" out loud. In fact, I enjoy this so much that I encourage the rest of the congregation to try the same thing. And I will probably continue to ask it. The difference is that now I have a little better understanding of the many moods and circumstances each of us brings to a worship service. Some days are a "foot stomper," other times it may painful to be there at all.

The people of God come to worship God through praise, prayer and service. The God of love accepts these gifts, however they are offered.

Let us encourage and give thanks for the variety of expression in ourselves and others.

The following articles were written for the newsletter at Central United Methodist Church, Winona, Minnesota. Re-reading them in 2016, I discover a few changes in both theology and language that I would make now. However, by leaving the articles in their original form, the reader will have a window into theological change and language progress.

WORLD COMMUNION

Who in the World is My Neighbor?

This question has been in my thoughts for several days as I have wondered how to bring together "world" and "communion." The service of communion is one I look forward to as a joyful celebration of the resurrection and freedom found in Christ. The state of our world brings me thoughts of fear and frustration - where is the spirit of Christ in all of this? Does my faith and religious belief give any insights on reconciling these apparently opposite concepts - world and communion?

The gospel of Jesus Christ is a message of love and forgiveness - and surprise. Surely Peter was surprised when his vision (Acts 10:9ff) revealed to him that God accepted persons outside the Jewish faith. Was it a surprise to other apostles that Paul soon realized he must take the good news of Jesus to the "Gentiles" (persons other than the Jewish people)? Was it a surprise to Jesus' listeners when he said, "Love your enemy and pray for those who persecute you?"

What did the man who asked the question, "who is my neighbor?" think of the parable Jesus told when it indicated that the neighbor was a person Jewish people viewed as an enemy? Is it a surprise to us when we are confronted with Jesus' words, "For if you love those who love you, what reward do you have? Do not even the tax collectors do the same? And if you greet only your brothers and sisters, what more are you doing than others?" (Matthew 5:46-47). A surprise? A hard challenge is more like it!

I wonder if we continue to grow in our spiritual life if we are not invited or prodded to examine again what we say we believe. Is Jesus Christ the model for our lives? Are all people on earth God's children? I've been angry and upset with the leaders of national and world governments and churches for allowing a political situation to so quickly bring us close to war. But, in fairness to those others I so readily criticize, I must admit to being surprised at how quickly I lost my center of peace when I let anger and fear have the upper hand.

Where is peace to be found? In searching for an answer, I re-read a book by Peace Pilgrim. Two paragraphs can be applied to the current situation:

"All people can be peace workers. Whenever you bring harmony into any unpeaceful situation, you contribute to the total peace picture. Insofar as you have peace in your life, you reflect it into your surroundings and into your world.

"In a conflict situation you must be thinking of a solution which is fair to all concerned, instead of a solution which is of advantage to you. Only a solution which is fair to all concerned can be workable in the long run."

Can "world" and "communion" be combined? By all means! It is an invitation for me to bring to God not only the hurts and shortcomings of the world as I see them; more importantly, it is the opportunity for me to bring myself for the healing which this sacrament of communion offers. Let all of us join around the communion rail on October 7th, realizing once again our unity with the risen Christ and our world.

(9/28/90)

Advent

Again and Again

The Church's new year begins as we observe the first Sunday in Advent. Again, as we have done every other year, we follow the story of the life of Christ from prophecy to glorious resurrection. Advent, the season of preparation, has long been an important time in the Church. In the year 380 CE, a council in Spain decreed that "from December 17 until the day of Epiphany (January 6) no one is permitted to be absent from church." Important indeed!

But what decrees are there today? Our grace-centered faith tells us that we are not forced to be any place for a specified length of time; rather, we are offered an all-encompassing, all-forgiving Love which is the answer to everything we ever need or want.

Again and again, Christ is born to us.

Again and again, we are offered Love.

We come to worship services, not because we have to come, but we come out of love and thanksgiving for the gift of Christ, given to us again and again.

"And his name shall be called Emmanuel - God with us."

(11/25/87)

A Season of Hope

I have been touched by two tragedies recently - one, the death of a small infant; the other, the death of a 23 year old young man. Although only on the edge of these events, I have felt sadness for the persons involved. I wonder how many more times the scenes are played out across the country. Where is hope in the midst of death and destruction? Are the homeless, the hungry and the grieving asking the same questions as the ancient Hebrew people, "How long, Lord? How long before peace and justice? How long before hope?"

Many of us are not facing such calamities in our lives. We allow an "already full" schedule to escalate to "frantic" during the Advent/Christmas season. There is no time to ask "how long before hope?" The season of

Advent gives us another opportunity to come face to face with the needs of our lives, whether that need is from poverty, or grief, or from preoccupation with material wealth. We meet again the God who does indeed understand death as well as life, who offers the Son as hope for us and the whole world.

> Hope of the world, thou Christ of great compassion,
> speak to our fearful hearts by conflict rent.
> Save us, thy people, from consuming passion,
> who by our own false hopes and aims are spent.
> Hope of the world, God's gift from highest heaven,
> bringing to hungry souls the bread of life,
> still let thy spirit unto us be given,
> to heal earth's wounds and end all bitter strife.

> (Georgia Harkness)
> (11/22/89)

Epiphany

Have You Found the Star?

Much of my career has been spent serving a church in a neighboring state. This meant that since I was responsible for playing/directing the Christmas Eve services, I could never be with my family until late Christmas afternoon. One year, the weather forecast indicated that travel might not be possible on Christmas day.

I spent several hours feeling very sorry for myself that work and weather might combine to prevent my travel on such a special day. Although I told some of my friends that it wouldn't make much difference whether I left on Christmas or the day following, I suddenly found myself in tears as I realized that it did matter. Then the unexpected happened: through the weeping came the thought: Weep for those who have no family, weep for those who have no home. Tears of sadness quickly turned to tears of gratitude that the Spirit (or my angel, perhaps) could break through my self-centeredness and give me comfort as well as re-direction.

The day of Epiphany is our opportunity to celebrate once again that Jesus Christ came into the world for all peoples. He still comes to us in our weeping and in our laughter.

Are we looking for His star?

Are we listening for His voice?

Will we let God use our sadness and joy as a channel to help the Kingdom come on earth?

The last stanza of "We Three Kings" reminds us of the triumph of Christ:

> Glorious now behold him arise;
> King and God and sacrifice: Alleluia, Alleluia,
> sounds through the earth and skies.

(1/4/91)

LENT

Giving Up

Many of us will remember an earlier time when friends and neighbors, especially those who were Roman Catholic, "gave up" something during Lent. Protestants may have made fun of this custom by proclaiming, "I'm giving up asparagus" or something equally as silly.

The original intent of making a sacrifice in order to identify more with Christ's sacrifice somehow got lost in the shuffle of ordinary living. More modern religious thought suggests that we think of "adding on" or "doing something special" during the season, rather than giving up anything.

These phrases encourage us to take time to look honestly at ourselves and resolve to more nearly reflect

God's love in our lives. "Giving up" is at the heart of the Church's story: Jesus Christ trusted God so completely that He gave up His spirit into the hands of a loving Creator, knowing that death was not the end. Faith in Christ gives us the assurance that God never "gives up" on us - Hallelujah!

(3/10/88)

What Shall We Do With Him?

We hear Pilate's question: "Then what do you wish me to do with the man you call the King of the Jews?" And we hear the response: "Crucify him!"

The same question remains today: What shall we do with Jesus?

What shall we do with the man and his ideas about love and forgiveness?

What shall we do with the man who said not to strike back but turn the other cheek instead; who advised his followers to "love your enemies and pray for those who persecute you, so that you may be children of your Father in heaven"?

What shall we do with the idea of forgiving another not just seven times, but seventy-seven times?

What shall we do with the supreme act of forgiveness - Jesus' words from the Cross, "Father, forgive them, for they do not know what they are doing"?

Jesus Christ's message of love and forgiveness is as radical today as it was two thousand years ago.

What shall we do with Him? The world still cries "Crucify him!"

Do we who claim to be his followers dare to cry "Crown him Lord of all!"?

(3/1/91)

EASTER

Who's Coming to Dinner? Guess!

One of my favorite scripture passages is the Road to Emmaus story. This is the account of two disciples walking toward Emmaus the afternoon of the Resurrection—but they didn't know that Jesus has risen. A stranger joins them as they walk and the conversation turns to the events of the past few days. The stranger points out how those events have fulfilled the writings of the prophets of Israel and the men seem not to question how he could know all of this.

As they arrive at their destination, the two disciples invite the stranger to come in with them and share a meal. The scriptures tell us that when the stranger picked up the bread and cup and gave thanks, "Their eyes were opened and they knew Him!" The risen Christ was in their midst!

Is the risen Christ in our midst? The Church throughout all the ages has answered with a resounding, "Yes!"

The season of Eastertide – the Sundays between Easter and Pentecost – is a time to especially focus our attention on the Resurrection. Come, add your "Yes" to the voices of our congregation – see you in church!

(4/30/1987)

Ordinary Time

Ho-Hum

The times of penitence, the days of celebration - all those special occasions which began with the season of Advent last November are over. Now comes the time the Roman Catholic calendar calls "ordinary time." It seems appropriate that this occurs during the summer months - those months in which we get away from the schedules and demands of the winter months or the school calendar or the stress of our jobs. We all need "ordinary time" in our lives for rest, recreation and recharging.

Ah... You've already guessed where this is leading. That's right - there really is nothing ordinary about the gospel, the good news that God loves and accepts us. Is anything more extraordinary?!

The season of "ordinary time" is another gift from our Creator, another opportunity for us to grow in our own spiritual understanding and also to be channels of God's love to others. See you in church!

(7/8/87)

The following articles were written for publications of Urbandale United Church of Christ, Urbandale, Iowa.

A Few of My Favorite Things
Isaiah 2:1-5

The Choir and I have a running joke about my "favorite anthem" - they hear me use that adjective on many of the pieces we prepare for worship services. It may be an especially poignant text, or a beautiful musical phrase, or a special association; whatever the reason, the anthem is on my "favorites" list.

The first Sunday in Advent, one of my favorite days, invites us to begin the anticipation and celebration of the arrival of Jesus yet one more time. I look forward to the whole season—to the hope that comes through the scripture, to the comfort that comes through the music.

In the scripture lesson for today, Isaiah lays out the picture for us immediately: God will judge the nations and the response is that "they shall beat their swords into plowshares, and their spears into pruning hooks."

Is that message of hope and peace still possible today? Despair and hopelessness grip our hearts. Yet the gospel continues to herald the profound message: We can live in hope. War and violence will end.

The anthem which the Choir sings on this first Sunday in Advent is a rather dramatic setting of the Isaiah text. Yes, it's one of my favorites, not only because of the words and music, but also because of the composer, Joseph Clokey. He wrote it after his son had been killed in World War Two. Imagine—suffering the terrible loss of a child and yet choosing to create music for a text which speaks of peace. What a statement of faith!

> Let us hope when hope seems hopeless,
> when the dreams we dreamed have died.
> When the morning breaks in brightness,
> hunger shall be satisfied.
> One who sows the fields with weeping
> shall retrace the sorrowing way
> and rejoice in harvest bounty
> at the breaking of the day.
>
> (David Beebe)

During this season of Advent, let us put hope and peace on our list of favorite things.

(11/28/04)

Ready or Not

Ready or not, here I come! I think about that childhood phrase as I fit together all the pieces of the Advent/Christmas season.

So much music, so little time to rehearse it. There is more music to celebrate this glorious season than can ever be learned by any choir.

Even though I intellectually know we can't do it all, my heart still wishes this season had more time in it. It may take me awhile to discover the obvious, but the truth finally surfaced one year:

Christmas comes, whether I'm ready or not.

And thank God this is so!

Left to myself, I might get so involved with small details that nothing would ever seem to be quite "right" or "ready" for the celebration - but God comes anyway.

Join me in singing praise to the God who dares to become one of us - ready or not.

(1/19/96)

The Extra Day

Today is the extra day in February we find on the calendar every four years. *Extra* may be defined as "more than is due, usual, or necessary," and *extraordinary* continues with "going beyond what is usual, regular, or customary." We might use either definition when we try to measure the great love of God against the sin and temptation in our lives.

How can such a generous gift be received when we know we have fallen short of living Christ's example in our lives? Intellectually, we may understand that God's grace is a free gift; in our hearts, we may still question how this can be. The season of Lent is another opportunity for us to practice the blessing of receiving this Love that is much more than "what is due or usual."

Hymns "Ah, Holy Jesus" (218), "O Love, How Vast, How Flowing Free" (209) and "My Song Is Love Unknown" (222) in the *New Century Hymnal* can be used as examples of how poets express the wonder of Grace.

(Lenten devotional booklet, 2/9/96)

Although the following article is written from the perspective of a church musician, other areas of ministry may find ideas or reminders.

The Care and Feeding
of the Church Choir

One of the most loyal and hard-working volunteer groups in any church is the choir. How do you take care of your singers? Many directors already know and use the following suggestions. Sometimes we need a gentle reminder.

Laugh, mostly at yourself. Lloyd Pfautsch, longtime director of choral studies at Southern Methodist University, suggested that one needed a choir member who would play off of the director's comments and jokes, a person who sensed the right time for the right comment. "Of course," said Pfautsch, "there may also be persons in the choir who think they are that person and don't realize they are not." (Dr. Pfautsch was right on both counts.)

The other good piece of advice about church music

came from my father. He was an easygoing man who loved to sing in the choir. One of the many directors who served that church turned out to be quite demanding in a rather belligerent way. His favorite pose was standing behind the piano and pounding on top of it as he shouted directions or criticism.

My father quietly reminded me to remember that most singers had worked a full day somewhere else before they came to church and were probably doing the best they could. A love of people and a light touch create a bond between conductor and singer and still allow for moments to speak with passion about the high calling of church music.

Establish your credibility. Patiently wait for the trust to develop. The last choir I served as a college student was much more flexible than the first one I worked with as a professional. I was surprised to find out my new choir wasn't used to singing with direction coming only from the organ bench. They didn't know that my "new" ideas were well thought out. Nor did they know that I am serious about the role of music leadership in the worship service.

I couldn't take up where the old director left off, and this is probably true no matter how many churches we serve or how much experience we bring. But the bonding is worth the wait! I will defend my choir against any and all, and I know they will do whatever I ask of them in a worship service—it doesn't get much better than that.

Forgive yourself as well as the singers. In my early professional years, I would get quite upset when the performance of an anthem in the worship service wasn't nearly as good as it had been in the last rehearsal. At some point, I discovered that I couldn't control all the factors that might come into play in any given service: the weather, key singers who are ill, and any number of other distractions which cause the anthem to not go well.

If I did my best to ensure a good presentation of the music, I didn't have to shoulder a lot of blame for a less-than-perfect rendition. Along with this process of forgiving myself, I discovered something more important—I didn't have to blame the choir members, either. Choirs want to do their best, and most recognize when they fall short. That is when they need the director's nurturing, not the director's blaming.

Little things mean a lot. Nurturing means I send letters to my choir three or four times a year to thank them for a special service, anthem or the extra time they have spent in a season. We can celebrate birthdays, bake Valentine cookies… the list is endless.

Receive as well as give. Part of my responsibility is

to care about the spiritual health of my singers. Much of this happens in the anthem and hymn texts that I choose. It also means being supportive in the various life situations of choir members. As worship leaders, we expect to do just that - lead.

Let us recognize that once in a while we are the ones who need the nurturing and comfort, and that the singers stand ready to provide it. To allow this to happen is to discover new insight into the meaning of Grace. It's well worth the risk.

You Needed to Be There

One of my friends encouraged me to tell some of the funny things that have happened to me through the years as a church musician. Choir members and I laughed heartily at these two incidents when they happened and even in memory. However, they may lose something for the reader in translation.

The second minister with whom I worked in Winona prided himself in recounting his ministerial journey, starting on the Iron Range of northern Minnesota with no one to help with office or custodial work; he did it all. Through the years his appointments finally moved him to Winona Central, at that time considered one of the plum appointments in the state. The congregation employed a full time associate minister, secretary, custodian and me, a three-quarter time organist/choir director. The minister had no experience with additional staff (many ministers at that time did not) so the journey with him was sometimes bumpy.

Over the years his theological and liturgical positions solidified. I found his preaching heavy on Law and light on Grace but I was able to use a lot of music I deemed appropriate for whatever church season we were in without too much flack from him.

His favorite service during the whole year was the Maundy Thursday ritual, perhaps the most sorrowful day for many Christians. To this day, I don't know why he wouldn't have put Easter at the top of his list of favorites, but back to the story.

He combined the Tenebrae (candles extinguished as the betrayal of Christ is read) with the Last Supper Upper Room reading. The unsuspecting acolytes who generally lit a couple of candles on Sunday mornings, found themselves with a ritual almost impossible to keep track of in the descending darkness.

The Choir and I had our own problems. The minister wanted the old hymn, "'Tis Midnight and On Olive's Brow," sung as soon as most of the candles had been extinguished. I remembered the hymn from my early days in the Methodist church but hardly anyone in the

Choir knew it. The first year, I played the hymn softly on the organ. Most of the Choir didn't get the pitch, so their singing faded out as we reached the end.

The next year I was determined to make a better go of it, and I knew the minister expected it. The Choir sat in the first two pews at the front of the sanctuary and I sat on the end of one row. They all had flashlights in order to really see the page, and I had a pitch pipe to get us started. Since all four parts started on different pitches, the trick for the singer was to know where the beginning sound was in relation to his/her starting pitch.

In hindsight, I must not have been clear with each voice part on how to get their starting note from the pitch pipe. Boldly, I gave the signal to begin, and immediately we knew something was wrong. And the longer we sang, the more wrong it was!

There was a 20th century composer, Charles Ives, who often wrote his music in two keys at the same time. We were performing classical music and didn't know it! Various choir singers began to drop out. I still have this image of a couple of altos at the end of the pew shaking because they were laughing so hard, yet not daring to make a sound.

Somehow the service mercifully came to an end. As the Choir and I reached the bottom of the stairs and walked down the hallway to the Choir room, gales of laughter broke out.

The minister didn't speak to me for several days. I honestly don't remember if I apologized to him after the service or not. I came to the conclusion, a number of years into my work with him, that, at least to me, he seemed to behave in a passive-aggressive way. At that time, personality conflicts and psychological traits were not dealt with in the Church.

One other amusing thing. One of the musically untrained folks in the pews on that fateful night commented to one of the Choir members, "I don't think the Choir sounded quite right tonight."

Truer words were never spoken.

I retired from Urbandale United Church of Christ June 2011. I was pressed back into service when one of the elderly altos passed away that August. The family requested that the Choir sing. This is not the first time they have done that, but it was to be the first time when the casket would be right in front of them (it's a rather small Chancel, so they have to stand on the Chancel steps to sing). I needed to explain that this was a UCC congregation, so the general approach to things was more laid back than in a liturgical setting.

I met with the funeral director a couple of days before the service so we could discuss the placement of the casket—allowing enough room around it for the Choir on the steps and the floral arrangements to the side. I happened to mention that we would be placing Mabel's robe on the Communion Table, along with a floral arrangement. We had done this for a couple of other deceased Choir members.

At that point, the funeral director said, "Often we have requests to have a robe or gown on display so we have invested in a headless mannequin. You are welcome to use it."

The image of dear Mabel standing alongside the Choir in the form of a headless dress dummy was hilarious to me. I believe I kept my composure and simply gave an unassuming "thanks-but-no-thanks" response. However, the director gave us a gift he didn't realize— humor!

Retelling this episode to Choir members before the service was the light touch they and I needed in our grief as we prepared to sing Mabel into heaven.

About the author

Elsie P. Naylor, a native of Des Moines, IA, received church music and organ performance degrees from Drake University. Her major study was done with the late Russell P. Saunders, and further coaching with Dr. John Ferguson. She retired in 2011 after 44 years in the field of church music. Her first position was Director of Music/Organist for a large United Methodist congregation in Winona, Minnesota, where she developed a handbell program and an extensive Sacred Fine Arts Series. After 28 years, she returned to Des Moines and assumed the position of Music Program Director for the Urbandale United Church of Christ in 1996.

She was instrumental in the commissioning of several pieces of music: a set of organ variations on English hymn tunes by John Ferguson; handbell compositions by Cynthia Dobrinski and Hart Morris; and choral anthems by Margaret Tucker and Craig Phillips.

In 1997 she established the Des Moines Diversity Chorus, a community group dedicated to affirming the worth of all people and cultures through music. Currently she serves on the Green Boat Crew at the Urbandale Church, a group committed to environmental justice. Ms. Naylor is also involved with the Des Moines Faith Committee for Peace.

Made in the USA
Lexington, KY
12 September 2017